TROPICAL
CLIMATES

Cath Senker

raintree

Raintree is an imprint of Capstone Global Library Limited, a company incorporated in England and Wales having its registered office at 7 Pilgrim Street, London, EC4V 6LB – Registered company number: 6695582

www.raintreepublishers.co.uk
myorders@raintreepublishers.co.uk

Edited by Linda Staniford
Designed by Philippa Jenkins
Original illustrations © Capstone Global Library Limited 2017
Illustrated by Oxford Designers and Illustrators
Picture research by Svetlana Zhurkin
Production by Steve Walker
Printed and bound in India

ISBN 978-1-4747-3837-8 (hardback)
20 19 18 17 16
10 9 8 7 6 5 4 3 2 1

ISBN 978-1-4747-3841-5 (paperback)
21 20 19 18 17
10 9 8 7 6 5 4 3 2 1

British Library Cataloguing in Publication Data
A full catalogue record for this book is available from the British Library.

Acknowledgements
We would like to thank the following for permission to reproduce photographs: Alamy: David Gee, 34, Renato Granieri, 28, Rolf Nussbaumer Photography, 20, Simon Rawles, 32; Capstone: Oxford Designers and Illustrators, 7, 12; Newscom: Danita Delimont Photography/Art Wolfe, 45, Danita Delimont Photography/Charles O. Cecil, 15, EPA/Stringer, 38, Eye Ubiquitous, 22, NHPA/Anthony Bannister, 41, NHPA/Martin Harvey, 24, ZUMA Press/KM Asad, 43; Shutterstock: Abhindia, 16, Andrew V Marcus, 39, AZP Worldwide, 40, brodtcast, cover, Chris Humphries, 17, elwynn, back cover and throughout, Eric Isselee, 26, ESB Essentials, 25, ESB Professional, 30, Fotos593, 5, gopfaster, 8, Gwoeii, 9, iofoto, 19, JustinDutcher, 11, Kelly Marken, 13, liewluck, 10, Magdalena Paluchowska, 27, Matthieu Gallet, 18, Oksana Byelikova, 29, Pawel Pietraszewski, 35, Rich Carey, 21, 36, Rudy Umans, 14, Sura Nualpradid, 44, Thinglass, 33, VEK Australia, 42, worldswildlifewonders, 37, Zzvet, 23

We would like to thank Dr Sandra Mather, Professor Emerita, Department of Geology and Astronomy, West Chester University, West Chester, Pennsylvania, USA, for her invaluable help in the preparation of this book.

CONTENTS

Some words are shown in bold, **like this**. You can find out what they mean by looking in the glossary.

WHERE ARE THE TROPICAL CLIMATES?

The tropical regions form a band around the Equator, between the Tropic of Cancer and the Tropic of Capricorn. South and Central America have vast rainforests. In Asia, the rainforests reach from India in the west to Borneo in the east. Australia has dense rainforests too.

But tropical climates aren't all the same. Some are hotter and damper than others. Close to the Equator, the climate gets wetter. The driest parts are the tropical deserts at the northern and southern edges of the tropics.

This map shows the tropical zones that lie around the Equator.

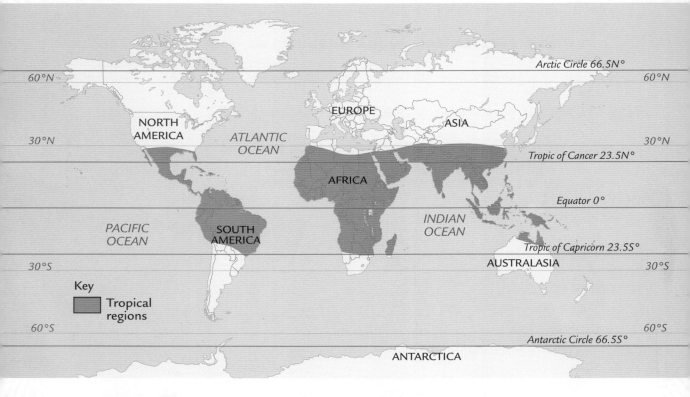

Arctic Circle 66.5N°

60°N

EUROPE

ASIA

NORTH AMERICA

30°N

ATLANTIC OCEAN

Tropic of Cancer 23.5N°

AFRICA

Equator 0°

PACIFIC OCEAN

SOUTH AMERICA

INDIAN OCEAN

Tropic of Capricorn 23.5S°

AUSTRALASIA

30°S

Key

Tropical regions

60°S

Antarctic Circle 66.5S°

ANTARCTICA

Amazing fact

The Amazon rainforest in South America is the largest in the world. It's twice the size of India.

The Amazon rainforest spans nine countries in South America.

LOW LATITUDES

The Sun is always strong and sometimes shines directly on these regions. There are tall tropical trees, amazing plants that **digest** insects, and colourful creatures, large and small. **Indigenous** people live deep in the remote rainforest as well as loggers, ranchers and miners.

DID YOU KNOW?

At the Equator, day and night are of almost equal length all the year round. The Sun rises at about 6 a.m. and sets at roughly 6 p.m. every day.

WHAT ARE TROPICAL CLIMATES LIKE?

TROPICAL RAINFORESTS

It never gets very cold in the tropical rainforests, even at night. The temperature is usually between 20° Celsius (68° Fahrenheit) and 32°C (90°F), but it can get up to 38°C (100°F). That's pretty hot and steamy!

The winds bring moisture to the land. Close to the Equator, the tropical rainforest regions are the wettest on the planet. They have 1,000 centimetres (400 inches) of rainfall a year – more than eight times as much as New York City. It rains all year round. That's why the rainforests are so dense and lush. Thunderstorms might be a rare, exciting event for many people, but in the rainforests they happen nearly every day.

This graph shows the temperature and rainfall in Belize, Central America.

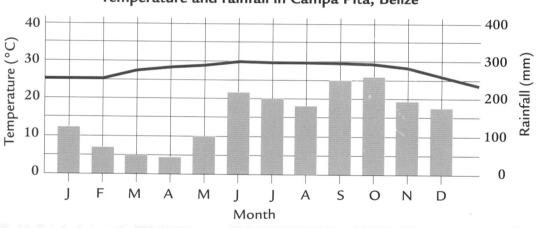

Temperature and rainfall in Campa Pita, Belize

TROPICAL MONSOONS

Some areas of the tropics, such as southern Asia or West Africa, have a tropical **monsoon** climate. Heavy rains fall in these regions during the monsoon season, which lasts up to three months in the summer. There may be violent thunderstorms here too. People in the tropics regularly have to cope with heavy rain, strong winds, flooding and mudslides.

Amazing fact

Sub-Saharan Africa covers almost 24 million square kilometres (over 9 million square miles). More than half of this area is tropical savannah.

This map shows where the three kinds of tropical climates occur: tropical rainforest, tropical monsoon and tropical savannah.

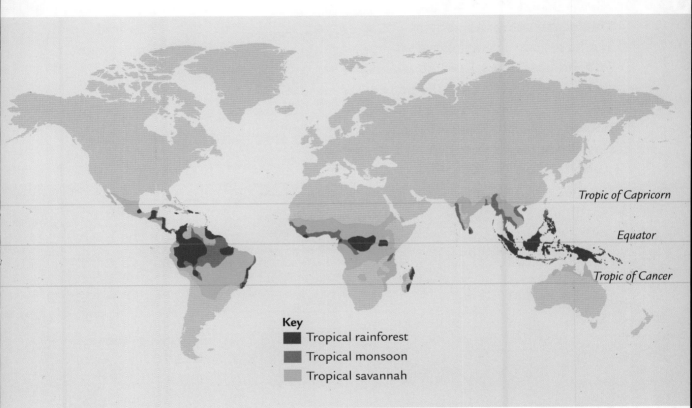

Tropic of Capricorn

Equator

Tropic of Cancer

Key
- ■ Tropical rainforest
- ■ Tropical monsoon
- ■ Tropical savannah

TROPICAL SAVANNAH

The tropical **savannah** lies further away from the Equator. The tropical savannah has three seasons: cool and dry; hot and dry; and hot and wet. It's usually warm, but the temperature varies during the year. The wet season here is shorter than in areas with a monsoon climate and there's less rain – although there are still heavy downpours.

A CHILLY CLIMB

Tropical regions are not hot everywhere. **Altitude** is an important influence on climate. Generally, as the land rises, the temperature drops by 1°C (1.8°F) every 100 m (328 feet). At sea level there are tropical rainforests and **mangroves**, but as the land rises above 900 metres (about 3,000 feet), these are replaced by montane (mountain) forests. As in the cooler climates, these forests have deciduous trees, which lose their leaves in winter. On the mountain peaks, there is even snow.

A traveller walks up a steep trail in the mountain forest of Khun Jae National Park, Thailand.

DID YOU KNOW?

Winds influence the climate. Trade winds blow from the north or south towards the Equator. These warm breezes blow nearly all the time. In the Northern Hemisphere, they blow from the north-east and in the Southern Hemisphere, from the south-east. The trade winds meet in the tropics. As they rise, they cool, creating clouds and heavy rainfall. They bring thunderstorms and warm, damp weather.

The altitude affects rainfall too. As moist air rises over a mountain, it cools. Clouds form and it rains. By the time the air reaches the other side of the mountain, it has lost its moisture. Little rain falls – this side is in what is called a rain shadow.

A massive storm brews over a tropical mountain. The wet-weather system comes from the ocean.

WHICH PLANTS LIVE IN TROPICAL REGIONS?

TROPICAL RAINFORESTS

Rainforest trees are evergreen; that is, they keep their leaves all through the year. Their broad leaves form a dense covering, shading the forest floor.

The trees have special ways of coping with the damp climate. Their bark is thin and smooth. They don't need thick bark to stop them from drying out, because it's always damp in the rainforest. Their roots are shallow, because there is no need for roots to stretch deep underground to access water. Near the base of their trunks are large, branching ridges. These are buttresses, or supports, to hold up the tree. Without the buttresses, the trees would topple over. The buttresses rise 9 m (30 feet) high and then blend into the trunk.

Rainforest leaves have drip tips to stop them from rotting in the damp environment.

Drip tips

The leaves have "drip tips" to help water drip off so they don't stay wet, which would allow **bacteria** and fungi to grow. The surface of the leaves is waxy so the water runs off quickly.

Amazing fact

Rainforests are one of Earth's oldest habitats. Some forests in South-east Asia were there at least 100 million years ago, when the dinosaurs were alive!

DID YOU KNOW?

Plants need light to survive, but the dense forest is dark. **Epiphytes** have a cunning solution. They live high up on the surface of other plants, especially tree trunks and branches, so they can access sunlight in the canopy. Epiphytes include orchids, bromeliads and ferns.

Mangroves

Close to the sea in tropical **deltas** and estuaries, where rivers flow into the sea, rainwater cannot flow away easily. Mangroves line the edges of the waterways. The trees have adapted to the marshy land. Stilt roots hold them up in the mud.

TROPICAL RAINFOREST ZONES

Tropical rainforests have four zones, and plants are specially adapted to live in each one.

Amazing fact

Some rainforest plants eat animals! On the pitcher plant vine, small pitchers (jugs) full of nectar attract insects. When the insects try to drink the nectar, they fall in and the plant digests them.

Emergent layer
The tallest trees grow in the top layer. They tower above the canopy trees to reach the sunlight.

Canopy
Here, many tall trees form a roof over the lower layers. Up to 90 per cent of rainforest plants and animals have their homes in the canopy.

Understorey
Young trees and leafy plants grow in the shade of the canopy. Many popular house plants originally came from the rainforest understorey.

Forest floor
In some places, the forest floor only receives 2 per cent of the sunlight. Here, only plants that can cope with very little light can survive. There are also fallen leaves, fruit and seeds.

DID YOU KNOW?

Pineapples are a familiar example of a bromeliad. There are more than 3,000 species of bromeliads. Some, such as pineapples, grow in plants above the ground, but others grow on rocks and on other plants and trees where it's easier to access sunlight. Sometimes, so many bromeliads grow on a branch that it collapses under the weight. The leaves of a bromeliad form a "vase" that holds water. As well as bacteria, many species are found in these "vases", including mosquitoes, dragonflies, birds, frogs and salamanders.

TROPICAL MONSOON CLIMATE

Moving away from the Equator, the climate changes to a monsoon climate. Where the monsoon winds bring the heaviest rain, there are thick forests, such as in southern Myanmar, northern Australia and parts of India. But the forest is less dense than tropical rainforests and has fewer species. Tropical monsoon forests have three layers – there's no emergent layer. Because the rain is seasonal, there are deciduous trees. In the rainy season, the trees grow rapidly. They shed their leaves in the dry season to save energy and preserve water.

TROPICAL SAVANNAH

In the drier tropical savannah, there are wide expanses of grassland scattered with trees. But the grasses aren't like a neat garden lawn. Elephant grass can grow up to 3 m (10 feet) tall!

The Everglades, USA has a tropical savannah climate. Water flowing through the region supports a wide range of animals, fish and birds.

Palm, pine and acacia trees, and shrubs grow here. They make good use of the moisture and can cope with long periods of **drought**. Their tap roots (long, thick roots growing downwards) can reach the **water table**. The trunks store the water, and thick bark slows down **evaporation**. Thick bark also helps the plants to resist damage when wildfires rage through the grasslands.

Amazing fact

Eucalyptus or gum trees grow in the Australian savannah. The giant gum grows more than 90 m (300 feet) high – as tall as a 27-storey building.

DID YOU KNOW?

Many savannah plants have edible fruit, flowers or seeds. But it is important to know what to look for and be able to recognize which plants are safe to eat. These plants offer tasty treats:

Abal Flowers with a high sugar content

Acacia Edible leaves, flowers and pods

Baobab (shown right) The root, fruit pulp and leaves are edible, and the seeds are ground to make flour

Beech Tasty nuts

Wild melon Very juicy and thirst quenching

WHICH ANIMALS LIVE IN THE TROPICAL REGIONS?

TROPICAL RAINFOREST ANIMALS

Tropical rainforests are noisy places. A variety of animals call to each other, swing from branch to branch or buzz around looking for food.

About a quarter of the world's bird species live in rainforests. Birds such as parrots and toucans feed on fruit and seeds, and later their droppings fall to the forest floor. Seeds inside the droppings grow into new plants.

Many other animals are adapted to the high life in rainforest trees. Mammals, reptiles and **amphibians** live in the canopy, feeding mostly on the delicious fruits that grow there. Some animals never even go down to the forest floor.

A bright blue poisonous frog. Poison-dart frogs are among the most toxic animals in the world.

Warning colours

Many creatures are brightly coloured to warn predators to keep away because they taste bad. Poisonous frogs come in a rainbow of colours – red, orange, yellow or with bright green or blue patterns. Their skin produces poison so toxic it can kill a person. Indigenous South American people coat the tips of their arrows with the poison to hunt birds or monkeys for food.

Amazing fact

Tropical rainforests contain half of the plant and animal species on Earth.

Leopards often store their kill in a tree to hide it from other predators.

Fierce prowlers

Tigers, jaguars and leopards lurk in the rainforests. The markings on their coats camouflage them so they are hard to spot. Tigers are large and strong, feared by all other creatures. Jaguars and leopards are agile climbers that can pursue their prey into the trees. Jaguars are good swimmers too. A jaguar can chase its meal into the river.

DID YOU KNOW?

Insects form the largest group of animals that live in tropical rainforests. There are huge ant colonies, many varieties of bright butterflies, stick insects (insects that look like twigs) on the tree branches and millions of mosquitoes.

ON THE SAVANNAH

Lions, leopards, hyenas and jackals roam the grasslands on the hunt for giraffes, zebras and buffaloes for dinner.

Grass feeders

Elephants also live on the African savannah. They feed on grasses, fruit, leaves, bark and shrubs. Predators find it hard to attack these giants, and elephant skin is tough to bite. The whole herd protects the more delicate young calves from danger.

Elephants live in herds for protection; females often stay with their mother until she dies.

Hoofed mammals are well suited to savannah life. Many kinds of antelope feed on the grasses, thrusting their huge tongues forward to graze the vegetation. They have keen senses of smell and hearing. If they detect a lurking leopard, they race away to safety. Thomson's gazelle can run at speeds of up to 80 kilometres (50 miles) per hour – as fast as a family car on a main road!

Digging underground

In some tropical grasslands, mice, moles, gophers and ground squirrels dig burrows under the ground to hide themselves from predators. Worms, termites and beetles make their homes here too.

Australian animals

The Australian savannah has its own unique animals, mostly marsupials (animals that carry their young in pouches) such as kangaroos and koalas. Koalas are fussy eaters. They only eat eucalyptus leaves. Koalas have strong claws for climbing up the trunks of eucalyptus trees and rough paws for gripping the branches.

A koala bear in Australia feeds on eucalyptus leaves.

? DID YOU KNOW?

The savannah grasslands are ideal feeding grounds for snakes. They hunt for small animals in the trees and on the ground. The black mamba lives in the savannah of South Africa. It's the deadliest snake in the world. Growing up to 4 m (14 feet) long, it strikes voles, rats or squirrels, paralyses them so they cannot move, and eats them whole.

ORANG-UTANS IN THE OIL PALMS

Across Borneo, oil-palm plantations have been planted for the food industry, which uses the oil in hundreds of snack foods and toiletries. The plantations have rapidly replaced the native rainforests, and around 80 per cent of the orang-utan habitat has disappeared during the last 20 years. Oil-palm plantations contain trees, as rainforests do, but researchers have found that some of the orang-utans there are starving. Why aren't the orang-utans doing well in the oil-palm forests?

An orang-utan eats fruit, part of its normal diet, in Putting National Park, Borneo, south-east Asia.

MISSING HOME FOOD

Researchers found that orang-utans in their native Kinabatangan forest in Borneo enjoy a varied diet of more than 300 plant species. They eat leaves, bark and insects, and are particularly fond of figs and durian fruit – the durian smells disgusting,

but is delicious. Yet orang-utans have trouble with oil-palm fruits; they cannot digest them properly, and they do not thrive on just one type of food. It would be like people living on pasta alone. It might seem fine at first, but they would soon become bored of eating the same thing and grow ill.

An oil-palm plantation stands beside cleared rainforest in Borneo.

TRYING TO ADAPT

Although orang-utans are usually at home swinging through the trees, researchers found that orang-utans do a lot more walking on the ground in the oil-palm forests. Because they can do this, they are able to adapt to man-made landscapes where the trees are not as close together as in the rainforest. They have even started to make nests in oil-palm trees. It seems that the orang-utans are trying to adapt to the new habitat, but they cannot cope with the lack of variety in their diet.

DID YOU KNOW?

Orang-utan conservation groups are working to build "orang-utan bridges" in Borneo. Made from tough polyester, the bridges allow orang-utans to move between areas of the rainforest that have been cut off from each other by oil-palm plantations, roads and rivers.

WHO LIVES IN TROPICAL REGIONS?

The tropical rainforest is home to many indigenous peoples. Some of these include the Penan of Sarawak, Malaysia, the Yanomami of Brazil, the Pygmies of central Africa and the Kuku-Yalanji of north-eastern Queensland, Australia.

Indigenous people in the North-west Amazon, in Colombia, have cleared a small area of rainforest to grow their crops.

SUSTAINABLE SOCIETY

These indigenous peoples live deep within the rainforest, and outsiders can only find them with the help of guides. They live in tune with the forest in the traditional way, gathering just enough fruit, nuts, seeds and firewood for their needs. Rainforest soils are not very **fertile**, so farmers burn down small patches to grow crops for only a short while. Then they move on to grow crops in a different area so the soil can recover and the forest will grow back. It's a **sustainable** way of life for small numbers, but in many places, the traditional ways are dying out. People have come into contact with modern society, and young people in particular want to adopt a Western lifestyle.

These terraced rice fields are in Yunnan province, China. In winter, water is channelled from the top of the hill to irrigate the rice crop.

MONSOON FARMERS

The tropical monsoon regions are full of farmers. Here, water-loving crops thrive. People grow food crops such as rice, sugar, spices and vegetables, as well as cotton and bamboo. The crops are grown on flat areas called terraces that are cut into the hillside. The terraces help to conserve water while the seeds are sprouting.

People who live there cope with the heavy downpours when the monsoons arrive by building overhanging eaves so water flows away from their houses. The streets have deep, wide drains to collect the rain and prevent flooding.

 DID YOU KNOW?

Some indigenous groups remain isolated from the outside world. Nearly all of them are in the Brazilian rainforest. They may have had some contact with modern civilization, but it might have been negative. For example, their people might have been killed or made slaves. Usually, they keep their distance because they're afraid of being harmed.

RAINFOREST MIGRANTS

The riches of the rainforest attract **migrants** from the crowded cities hoping to make a living and big businesses looking to make a fortune. Unfortunately, the newcomers are destroying rainforest habitats.

Farmers plant crops on a newly cleared area of rainforest in Madagascar. Farmers here usually grow rice for a couple of years, leave the land fallow for four to six years, then repeat the process. After two or three plantings, the soil usually has no nutrients left.

Slash-and-burn farming

In the African and South American rainforests, farmers cut down and burn the vegetation so they can plant crops for food and fuel. At first the crops grow well. But tropical soils are of poor quality. When plants or animals die, they rot quickly in the warm, damp environment so soil doesn't stay fertile for long. Heavy rains wash away **nutrients** too. After a couple of years, the farmers leave to clear another area of forest. With large numbers of farmers in one area, this kind of agriculture is not sustainable.

Farmers are not alone in creating problems in the rainforest. Ranchers cut down vast areas of rainforest to raise cattle. It's a profitable business. Around the world, more and more people are demanding beefburgers and other beef products.

Logging and mining

Loggers chop down trees for timber. In Malaysia, Borneo and the Philippines, much of the forest has been cleared. In Brazil, plantations grow non-native eucalyptus to supply the paper industry. In Africa, Indonesia and South America, miners dig for gold, silver and iron ore. They use poisonous chemicals in the mining process, which can kill animals and plants in the area. It's not surprising the rainforests are in serious danger.

DID YOU KNOW?

Fuel for vehicles can be made from palm-tree fruit, soya beans and rapeseed. These biofuels cause less pollution and carbon dioxide emissions than **fossil fuels.** Yet, when farmers cut down the rainforests to grow these crops, it is bad for the environment.

TROPICAL SAVANNAH

The grasslands are covered with native grasses that provide food for cattle. On the African savannah, most people are farmers who keep livestock and grow crops.

Farmers on the savannah grow crops that can survive long dry spells, such as the cereals millet, sorghum, barley and wheat. In central Africa, eastern Brazil and northern Australia, vast plantations growing cotton, sugarcane, coffee, oil palm and tropical fruits cover parts of the grasslands.

Maasai life

Some of the indigenous Maasai of Kenya and Tanzania are farmers who still live the traditional nomadic life. They travel with their cattle, sheep and goats from place to place to find water and grass for their animals to graze on. The Maasai trade some of their animals and keep some for food.

Sugarcane is grown as a foodstuff but also to make a biofuel called sugar-cane ethanol.

Amazing fact

Cotton is grown in huge plantations in many tropical regions, including China, India and Brazil. It is used all around the world. People wear cotton T-shirts, dry themselves with cotton towels and sleep on cotton sheets. Cotton makes up nearly half of all the fibre used to make clothes worldwide.

The Kenyan and Tanzanian governments are encouraging Maasai farmers to give up their **nomadic** lives and live in permanent settlements. But grazing cattle and goats in one place reduces the fertility of the grasslands and could turn them into desert. In Australia, farmers have established huge farms for raising cattle that have been specially bred to cope with the tropical climate. The cattle may munch or trample so much of the native vegetation that the plants begin to die out.

Maasai herders live the traditional way of life in Tanzania.

DID YOU KNOW?

The Maasai are famous worldwide for their vivid clothing and location near the popular game parks of Kenya and Tanzania. They have inspired fashion, music and sports shoes, but many have lost land and live in poverty. Nearly 60 per cent of Maasai children under 5 years old are malnourished because they don't have enough of the right kinds of food.

ECOTOURISM – MARA NABOISHO CONSERVANCY

Most indigenous peoples of the tropical savannah struggle to survive because of overgrazing. A few Maasai people have discovered a new, sustainable livelihood.

The Maasai Mara National Reserve is the heart of the Kenyan savannah. Extremely popular with tourists, hundreds of thousands visit the reserve every year to view the wildlife.

Next to the reserve is the Mara Naboisho Conservancy, an ecotourism project that does not harm the environment. Visitor numbers are strictly limited to reduce the human impact on the environment. Visitors can pitch their tents in the grasslands and wake up to see zebra peacefully grazing. Naboisho Camp Manager Roelof Schutte says, "Wildlife viewing here is unparalleled, it's like walking into a wildlife documentary; it's raw, it's real, and it touches one's soul."

Vistors can get within a few metres of the lions in the Mara Naboisho Conservancy.

Amazing fact

The Maasai Mara is home to lions, leopards, elephants, crocodiles and rhinos, and more than 450 species of birds.

The land for the conservancy comes from more than 550 Maasai landowners, who receive fees for its use. The project brings economic benefits to the community because many people have jobs within the conservancy. To preserve the indigenous way of life, tourists have to respect the customs of the Maasai people and not engage in activities that would damage their way of life.

A Maasai woman makes traditional jewellery for sale to tourists.

CONSERVING WILDLIFE

Since tourist numbers are low, the animals are not disturbed by large numbers of visitors. The Naboisho Conservancy provides a good income so people don't need to rely on intensive farming, which damages the savannah habitat. The conservancy controls the amount of livestock so that cattle and local wildlife do not compete for food. Providing a decent living standard for local people also reduces **poaching** and the illegal trade in wildlife products. The conservancy won the African Responsible Tourism Award in 2016.

WHAT RESOURCES ARE THERE IN THE TROPICS?

IN THE TROPICAL RAINFOREST

Every day most people probably eat something that has come from a rainforest. Chocolate is made with cacao from Latin America or Africa. Bananas come from a tropical country too.

Building with bamboo

Wood from the tropics is used for timber, firewood, charcoal and building materials. Inside homes, cupboards, doors or floors might be made from tropical trees. The bamboo forests are a rich resource too. Grown in many tropical countries, bamboo is very strong. It is so tough that it is used to make scaffolding for building skyscrapers in Hong Kong!

Plant products

Many parts of tropical plants find their way into industry and medicines. They are used as fibres, resins, dyes and plant essences. Rubber comes from the tropics too. These plant products are usually sold abroad to developed countries. They are turned into products such as rattan fibre for making baskets and vanilla pods for flavouring food.

Hong Kong workers put up scaffolding made from bamboo.

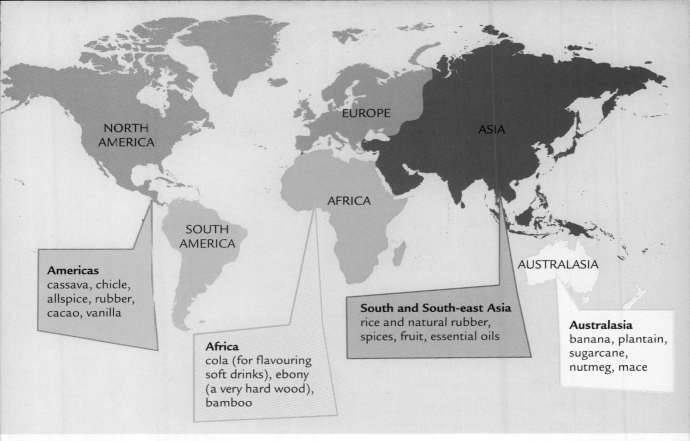

NORTH AMERICA

EUROPE

ASIA

SOUTH AMERICA

AFRICA

AUSTRALASIA

Americas
cassava, chicle, allspice, rubber, cacao, vanilla

Africa
cola (for flavouring soft drinks), ebony (a very hard wood), bamboo

South and South-east Asia
rice and natural rubber, spices, fruit, essential oils

Australasia
banana, plantain, sugarcane, nutmeg, mace

Minerals

The world's rainforests also have wealth underground, including gold, copper and diamonds. Bauxite is mined for making aluminium drink cans, and there's drilling for oil and gas in the western Amazon, in Colombia, Ecuador, Peru and Brazil.

 This map shows rainforest products from the world's tropical regions.

DID YOU KNOW?

Many medicines come from rainforests. Tropical snake venom (poison) makes the victim collapse due to a large drop in blood pressure. Scientists realized it could be used to make a drug to reduce dangerously high blood pressure. The Madagascar periwinkle plant can cure the most common childhood leukaemia, saving many young people from an early death.

FONCHO AND FAIRTRADE BANANAS

Many farmers in the tropics work long and hard all year round to grow their crops, but receive extremely low prices for them. Fairtrade is a global organization that works with businesses around the world to make sure farmers get a fair price for their crops.

THE FAIRTRADE FOUNDATION

The Fairtrade Foundation pays a minimum price for farm products. Farmers are better able to plan for the future because they know what price their products will fetch at the end of the season. In order to achieve the FAIRTRADE Mark, farmers must work in safe conditions. The farmers protect the forest environment so their activities are sustainable. Major Fairtrade products you can find easily in the shops are bananas, coffee, chocolate and sugar.

A banana farmer in Colombia checks on his crop.

More than one-third of bananas sold in the UK carry the Fairtrade mark.

BIGGER BUNCHES

Foncho is a banana farmer in Colombia who now sells through Fairtrade. Before doing this he made little money. With the extra cash he received from Fairtrade, he bought new equipment. He has **fertilizer** to strengthen the plants and water pipes for irrigation (watering). Each bunch now has more bananas.

Every day, Foncho gets up at 4 a.m. to check on the bananas. They take nine months to grow. After the bananas are picked, they are washed and inspected in the packing area. Perfect bananas of the right shape and colour are exported, while the rest are usually sold in Colombia.

With the extra income from Fairtrade, Foncho also bought a motorbike so his family could live in town. He drives to his farm every day. His 19-year-old daughter, Brenda, is the first in her family to go to college and has the chance of a well-paid job. His 15-year-old son, Sebastian, attends a good school – he loves sport and wants to be a physical education teacher. The Fairtrade Foundation has made a real difference to the life of Foncho's family.

IN THE TROPICAL MONSOON CLIMATE

Neem, banyan, acacia and eucalyptus are all broadleaved hardwood trees from tropical monsoon forests. All over the world, people use their hard, heavy wood to make beautiful furniture. Teak is particularly prized. It is used to build ships, fine furniture, and door and window frames.

Electricity from water

All that water from the monsoon rains is valuable too. Water can be used to produce electricity. In India and South-east Asia, energy from flowing water collected during the monsoon season is used in **hydro-electric power** (HEP) plants. They provide much of the electricity for homes, schools and businesses in the area. When the main summer rains are weak or late, there's less electricity available, and the price of power goes up.

Of course, the rains are vital for crops too, but it's a risky business depending on the monsoon rains for a living. Extremely heavy rain can damage buildings and ruin crops, while too little can lead to drought and cause plants to die.

This hydro-electric plant is in Himachal Pradesh, northern India. This state has many HEP projects.

Amazing fact

Tea is the oldest and most popular manufactured drink in the world. The biggest tea-producing country is China, which produced more than one-third of the world's tea in 2013. The next biggest producers are India, Kenya and Sri Lanka.

IN THE TROPICAL SAVANNAH

The tropical grasslands are rich in resources too. They provide trees for wood and water from major rivers. There's nutrient-rich soil for growing crops and grass for grazing livestock.

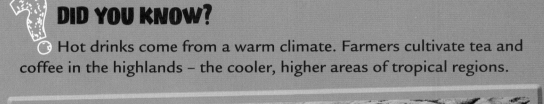

DID YOU KNOW?

Hot drinks come from a warm climate. Farmers cultivate tea and coffee in the highlands – the cooler, higher areas of tropical regions.

WHAT ARE THE THREATS TO THE TROPICAL REGIONS?

Deforestation, climate change and habitat loss are all serious threats to tropical regions. What is happening, and why does it matter?

RAVAGING THE RAINFORESTS

In the Amazon and eastern Africa, farmers cut down the forests to clear space for cattle ranching and farming, while loggers chop down trees for timber. Borneo and Sumatra have many oil-palm plantations, and in the Mekong region rubber, sugar, rice and crops grown for biofuels are replacing forests.

This tropical rainforest in Borneo is being destroyed to make way for an oil-palm plantation.

Amazing fact

Every second, a part of the rainforest the size of a football field is damaged or destroyed.

Habitat destruction

Cutting down forests destroys habitats. The tropical forests are home to the greatest variety of species in the world, but this region also has the highest number of endangered species. Some animals have already died out and others are under threat, including orang-utans, spider monkeys, crocodiles, gorillas and macaws. Deforestation affects indigenous peoples too. They lose their living space and the plants and wildlife they depend on.

Climate change

Deforestation contributes to climate change. The tropical climate has been stable for the last 3 million years, and rainforest plants and animals have adapted to the environment. Rising temperatures caused by **global warming**, along with changes in rainfall patterns, could lead to species dying out.

Spider monkeys in Costa Rica are severely endangered because of habitat loss.

DID YOU KNOW?

Trees and other plants photosynthesize – they make food from carbon dioxide in the air, water and sunlight. They store carbon dioxide. When they're cut down, they release the carbon dioxide into the **atmosphere**, which contributes to global warming. Deforestation causes about 15 per cent of global **greenhouse-gas emissions**.

MENACING MONSOONS

People who live in a monsoon climate are used to monsoon rains and rely on them for farming. But they have noticed that the rains are becoming more severe.

Disasters

Scientists predict that there will be heavier monsoon rains because of climate change. Stronger winds increase the size of the waves that batter the coast when there is a storm surge (an unusual rise in sea level caused by high winds from a big storm). Warming oceans produce heat to fuel tropical storms, and they are becoming more frequent and more intense. In India and Bangladesh, devastating floods wash away homes and crops, and farmers lose their livelihoods. The drinking water becomes mixed with sewage (waste from humans), and people fall ill.

A powerful cyclone hit Odisha in 2013, one of the worst-ever tropical storms in India.

Disease and damage

Water pollution from storms is not the only reason for disease. As temperatures rise and the monsoon season becomes longer and stronger, diseases that love warm, wet weather thrive. Malaria, a deadly tropical disease, can spread more easily and is likely to move to new areas.

Many people in tropical monsoon zones make their living from the land, and the majority of them are poor. Fierce storms and floods often damage farmland, so poor farmers are likely to suffer greatly from climate change.

TROUBLE IN THE TROPICAL SAVANNAH

The rich soils of the grasslands are good for agriculture, but poor farming practices damage the land.

Single-crop farming

Farmers hoping for bumper crop yields often plant single-crop plantations with one harvest of cotton, sugarcane or a cereal. This can cause problems:

1. Pests attack a crop and munch the seedlings.
2. Disease spreads through the crop.
3. Farmers spray the bugs with pesticides – chemicals that kill the pests but also useful insects.
4. The rains arrive, washing nutrients from the soil so the farmers have to buy fertilizer.
5. The following year, the same bugs attack the crop.

Single-crop farming decreases fertility, so the land becomes less and less productive. After a few years, little grows.

This sweetcorn crop is diseased. A single-crop plantation can quickly be destroyed when disease takes hold, which is why pesticides are so commonly used.

Overgrazing

The grasslands are an ideal habitat for herders, such as the indigenous Maasai, but large-scale ranching by big companies stresses the soil. Cattle overgraze the grasslands, and droughts make the problem worse. Grasses die, leaving only roots to hold the soil together. Wind erodes the soil in the dry season, and heavy rains wash it away during the wet season.

Habitat loss

Adding to the pressure on grasslands, people are destroying the natural habitat to build new towns, which makes climate change worse. Higher temperatures and irregular rainfall could turn grasslands into deserts, and we could lose them forever. This would also destroy the habitat of the animals that live on the grasslands, so they would become endangered or even die out.

In Ovamboland, Namibia, the large population of cattle at this ranch has overgrazed the grassland, putting pressure on the environment.

DID YOU KNOW?

Savannah elephants are the biggest land animals on Earth. They feed on leaves, bark and twigs, making the trees less dense and maintaining the grasslands, which helps other animals. But they're under threat from poaching because their tusks fetch a high price in the illegal ivory market.

HOW CAN WE PROTECT THE TROPICAL REGIONS?

Even if you live far away from the tropical rainforests, you can still do your bit to protect them. You can recycle aluminium cans so less bauxite is needed to make new ones. When you're out shopping, look for Fairtrade bananas, sugar and chocolate. Make sure any furniture your family buys has an FSC certificate, which means the wood comes from sustainable forests.

In the tropical savannah, farmers can rotate their crops to keep the soil fertile and plant trees as windbreaks to reduce soil erosion. Wildfires are natural in savannah regions and help to preserve the grasslands by stopping trees from growing. The burnt vegetation provides the soil with nutrients. How can we get the benefits of wildfires without the dangers?

Controlled burning in the Australian savannah reduces the amount of fuel available during the drier months when wildfires are likely.

Fire control

In the savannah region of northern Australia, wildfires occur regularly in the dry months and can rage through farms and put lives at risk. The indigenous Aboriginal people had ways of controlling the fires. They regularly burned some areas so that the vegetation on the grasslands didn't become too dense. Then when a wildfire did break out, there was less fuel and the fire burned with less heat and caused less damage. Some indigenous methods are now being combined with the latest science to carry out controlled burning in the savannah.

DID YOU KNOW?

In south Asia, simple methods can protect people from the effects of intense monsoon rain. In Bangladesh, the international charity Oxfam has introduced portable clay ovens (like the one shown below) that people can bring with them to high ground when they have to escape the floods. People plant gardens that float on top of the floodwater and place toilets on raised land so that waste won't enter the water and cause disease.

SAVING THE FORESTS

Scientists estimate that up to one-third of greenhouse-gas emissions could be stopped by halting deforestation in tropical rainforest regions and restoring forest land. Forests are a "carbon sink" (a natural environment that absorbs carbon dioxide from the atmosphere) and tropical forests store the most carbon. It would be far quicker to stop deforestation than to end the use of fossil fuels (another big source of greenhouse-gas emissions).

Volunteers plant young trees as part of a mangrove reforestation project in Samut Sakhon, Thailand.

Amazing fact

In the Andes Mountains, scientists have noticed that trees are migrating up the slope when they reproduce to escape warming temperatures. They are moving about 2.5–3.5 m (8–12 feet) upwards each year. Plants themselves are trying to outrun climate change!

Governments can set up protected areas to help native species to survive. Researchers investigated tropical regions where this has been done and found it really did help the wildlife. It's important to act against illegal logging too. Such measures need to be adopted permanently. All the countries of the world have an interest in helping tropical lands to save the forests in the interests of our planet.

This anteater is in Manú National Park, in the remote tropical forest of Peru. Here, plants and animals are protected, and the only permanent residents are indigenous people.

GLOSSARY

altitude height above sea level

amphibian animal that can live on land and in water

atmosphere layer of gases that surrounds Earth

bacteria tiny forms of life in the air, water and soil, and in dead creatures and plants, which are often a cause of disease

deforestation cutting down or burning the trees in an area

delta area where a river splits into smaller branches before entering the sea

digest when food is changed into substances the plant or animal can use

drought long period with little or no rain, leading to a shortage of water

epiphyte plant that grows on another plant

evaporation change of water from a liquid into a gas

fertile good for growing crops

fertilizer substance that farmers add to soil to make plants grow better

fossil fuel fuel such as coal or oil, which was formed over millions of years from the remains of animals or plants

global warming increase in the overall temperature of Earth's atmosphere

greenhouse-gas emissions when gases that warm Earth, such as carbon dioxide and methane, are released into the atmosphere

hydro-electric power (HEP) using the power of moving water to make electricity

indigenous (person) one of the original peoples of a land

mangrove tropical tree that grows in mud or at the edge of rivers and has roots that are above ground

migrant person or animal that moves to another part of the country or another land – this is called migration

monsoon wind that brings heavy rain and storms to tropical areas

nomadic moving from place to place in search of grazing land

nutrient substance that is vital for a plant or animal to live and grow

poaching illegally hunting animals on someone else's land

savannah flat, open area of land that is covered with grass but has few trees

sustainable way of doing things that does not destroy natural resources

water table level at and below which water is found in the ground

FIND OUT MORE

BOOKS

It's all about . . . Riotous Rainforests (Kingfisher, 2015)

The Tropical Rain Forest: Discover This Wet Biome, Philip Johansson (Enslow Elementary 2015)

Tropical Rain Forests, Leon Gray (Brown Bear Books, 2016)

Tropical Rainforests, Tim Harris (Franklin Watts, 2015)

Where on Earth? Rainforests, Susie Brooks (Wayland, 2015)

WEBSITES

www.bbc.co.uk/nature/habitats/Tropical_and_subtropical_moist_broadleaf_forests
Find out about rainforests around the world and the plants and animals that live in them.

www.bbc.co.uk/nature/habitats/Tropical_and_subtropical_grasslands,_savannas,_and_shrublands
Learn about grasslands around the world and the plants and animals that live in them.

environment.nationalgeographic.com/environment/habitats/rainforest-profile/
This site has lots of information about the rainforest.

PLACES TO VISIT

The Living Rainforest
www.livingrainforest.org/visit
Rainforest climates in tropical glasshouses

London Zoo
www.zsl.org/zsl-london-zoo
Tropical biomes, including a Gorilla Kingdom

Tropical Birdland
www.tropicalbirdland.com
A wide variety of tropical birds

INDEX